JUN 25 '04

Weddings

Paul Mason

Heinemann Library
Chicago, Illinois

© 2004 Heinemann Library
a division of Reed Elsevier Inc.
Chicago, Illinois

Customer Service 888-454-2279
Visit our website at www.heinemannlibrary.com

Designed by David Poole and Geoff Ward
Originated by Ambassador Litho Ltd
Printed in China by Wing King Tong

08 07 06 05 04
10 9 8 7 6 5 4 3 2 1

**Library of Congress Cataloging-in-Publication
Data**
Mason, Paul, 1967-
   Weddings / Paul Mason.
      p. cm. -- (Rites of passage)
Summary: Explains the origin, historical or religious
significance, and practice of marriage and weddings in
different cultures around the world.
Includes bibliographical references and index.
   ISBN 1-4034-3990-7 (lib. bdg.) -- ISBN 1-4034-2515-9
(pbk.)
   1. Marriage customs and rites--Juvenile literature. [1.
Marriage
customs and rites. 2. Rites and ceremonies.] I. Title. II.
Series.
   GT2665.M37 2003
   392.5--dc21

                    2003001900

Acknowledgments
The author and publisher are grateful to the following
for permission to reproduce copyright material:
Cover photograph Topham Picturepoint.
pp. 4, 16, 17 Nik Wheeler/Corbis; p. 5 Rex Features; p. 6
Kaluzny-Thatcher/Getty Images; p. 7 Louis Bencze/Getty
Images; p. 8 David Cumming/Corbis/Eye Ubiquitous; p. 9
Earl & Nazima Kowall/Corbis; pp. 10, 21 Alamy Images;
p. 11 Bob Krist/Corbis; p. 12 Charles & Josette Lenars/
Corbis; p. 13 The Hutchison Library; pp. 14, 15 Peter
Sanders; pp. 18, 19 Israel Talby/Israelimages.com; p. 20
M L Sinibaldi/Corbis; p. 22 Natalie Fobes/Corbis; p. 24
Corbis/Bettmann; p. 25 Reuters; p. 26 Mkhitar
Khachatrian/Armenian International; p. 27 The British
Library; p. 28 William Harrigan/Lonely Planet Images;
p. 29 Humanist Society.

Special thanks to Lynne Broadbent of the BFSS National
Religious Education Center at Brunel University,
England, for her help in the preparation of this book.

Some words are shown in
bold, **like this.** You can find out
what they mean by looking in
the glossary.

Contents

Why Do We Have Weddings?

A wedding is a special **ceremony** in which a man and a woman agree that they are a couple. Usually, they make this agreement in front of their families and friends. Once the ceremony is finished, the couple is married.

Getting married is one of the most important events in many people's lives. It marks a rite of passage between being part of one's parents' family and starting a life of one's own. Many people move into their own home only after they get married: until then they live with their parents.

*These people are celebrating a **Hindu** couple's wedding in Malaysia.*

Weddings are also important to bride's and groom's families. The husband becomes a part of his wife's family, and the wife becomes part of her husband's. For this reason, in many cultures, family members help decide who would be a good husband or wife for someone.

Sometimes, families use a marriage as a way to join two groups. For example, in the past the royal families of Europe used marriages between their children to link their two countries. They believed that these connections would make both countries stronger.

Here, people are entering a church for the wedding of pop star Paul McCartney and Heather Mills, in 2002.

Rites of passage

In 1909, Arnold van Gennep wrote about rites of passage. He created this term to mean events that mark important moments of change in a person's life. He said there are three changes in every rite of passage:
- leaving one group
- moving on to a new stage
- and joining a new group.

Weddings in the Christian Church

The **Christian** Church is divided into different groups. They include **Roman Catholic, Orthodox,** and **Protestant.** Weddings are slightly different in each group, but the basic purpose of the **ceremony** is the same. Once married, the couple can have children within the laws of their religion. They often also agree to raise their children as Christians.

The ceremony

The couple makes promises or **vows** in church, witnessed by friends and family. The groom, the man getting married, waits at the front of the church near the altar. Then, the bride's father or other family member brings her down the **aisle** of the church and the ceremony begins.

Traditionally, the bride's father takes her down the aisle to the waiting groom.

The ceremony is led by a religious leader who stands with the couple at the front of the church. The man and woman believe that they are making their promises to each other in the presence of God. They promise to care for each other, and to stay married for life.

Wedding reception

After they are married, it is traditional for the couple and their guests to have a meal together. This is called a wedding reception—a gathering where family and friends can greet the couple and extend good wishes. Wedding receptions cane be at any time during the day, from morning to evening.

White dresses

Christian brides usually wear white dresses. They first became popular during the late 1700s. In the late 1800s, white dresses became so popular that very few brides wore anything else. This remains the case today.

The bride at a Christian wedding raises her glass happily. Many Christian brides wear white on their wedding day.

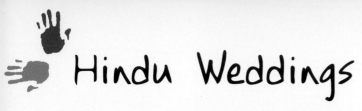

Hindu Weddings

About 80 percent of the people who live in India are **Hindus.** Hindus also live in many other parts of the world.

For many Hindu couples the first step in getting married is for the two families to agree on the arrangements. Sometimes the arrangements involve the bride's family paying a dowry. A dowry is a payment of money to the groom's family. The two families also agree on a wedding date and the arrangements for guests, food, and entertainment.

Music and songs

Music and songs—*sangeet* (san-jeet) and *geet* (jeet)— are important for a Hindu wedding. The celebrations are joyful and go on for several days. In the days before the **ceremony,** the women and girls of both families may join for a musical celebration. The women sing wedding songs and the girls dance. Sometimes, a professional singer is hired.

This Hindu bride is having her hand decorated with henna.

Hathleva

Hathleva (hat-lee-vah) is one name for a ceremony in which **henna** is put on the hands and feet of the couple getting married. Their hands are then tied together loosely with a scarf. This joining stands for the tie of marriage, which links a man and woman together forever.

The wedding ceremony

The bride and groom are seated in front of the **holy** fire. A *pundit* (religious teacher) leads the ceremony, making offerings to the holy fire and saying religious words. The couple walks around the fire three times, exchanging **vows.**

The bride and groom walk around a sacred flame as they exchange promises.

Sita Bibaha Panchami

This festival is held by people in the Kathmandu valley during November or December. The people hold mock wedding **processions** and celebrations in memory of the wedding of the goddess Sita and the god Rama.

Weddings in Punjab

In Punjab, a state in northern India, **Hindu** wedding customs are slightly different from those followed in other parts of the world. Once two families have agreed to a marriage, *roka* (rock-ah) takes place. Roka is a **ceremony** in which the bride and groom and their families get together, usually at the bride's house. Both families give the couple presents. Once *roka* is finished, the couple is **engaged.**

Sagan

The *sagan* (sag-an) ceremony happens on a day that is close to the actual wedding day. The bride's father puts a colored powder, usually red, called *tikka* on the grooms forehead, and the bride's family members bless him. The bride's family also gives presents. Between *sagan* and the wedding, the two families continue to celebrate together, singing and dancing at one each other's houses. One day may be set aside for *sangeet*, a musical celebration by the women of both families.

*A Hindu couple exchanges garlands of flowers. By now, some of the most important guests are getting hungry. This is because the bride, groom, and the bride's parents have all **fasted** for the whole day.*

For the wedding itself the bride is dressed in colors thought to be lucky, especially reds and oranges. The groom dresses in a light-colored suit and wears a turban.

The groom's family visits the bride's house for the *chunni chandana* ceremony. They give presents and jewelry to the bride. The groom and bride then exchange rings.

The wedding

The couple is married in a ceremony led by a *pundit.* The bride and groom and their parents go together. The bride's father puts a ring on the groom's finger. The groom's sister then ties the bride's clothes to the groom's. The couple is given milk and candy to celebrate the fact that they are now married.

Sikh Weddings

Sikh weddings are similar in many ways to **Hindu** ones. In many cases, two Sikh families help agree on a marriage arrangement. Sometimes, the bride's family visits the groom's to show that the agreement is settled properly. Then, the groom's family returns the visit, giving the bride clothes, a ring, and other jewelry.

Maiyan

Maiyan (may-ann) is a special Sikh custom. For several days before the wedding, the bride and groom are not allowed to go out, or even to change their clothes. The *gana* **ceremony** is then performed—a red thread is tied to the groom's right hand and the bride's left. The lucky-colored thread stands for a lucky marriage.

This Sikh couple is practically covered in flowers. They are getting married in India.

The night before the wedding, the bride's mother's family visits their relatives. They arrive singing and dancing, and at each stop some oil is added to the lamps they carry. When they have visited all of the relatives, the bride's hands and feet are painted with **henna** patterns.

The wedding day

In the morning, the bride and groom both have a ritual bath. Then they go to the **temple**. The morning **hymn** is sung, and then the couple and their parents stand and sing another short hymn. The couple agrees to be married by bowing to the *Siri Guru Granth Sahib,* the Sikh **holy** book. They walk four times around the book in a clockwise direction. The wedding ceremony ends with more singing.

This Sikh groom is wearing a sehra. *It covers the groom's face and is thought to be a form of protection against evil.*

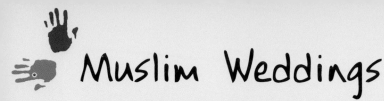

Muslim Weddings

A **Muslim** wedding can be a colorful event. Traditionally, it takes place over three days. The first celebration is called *Mehndi*. **Henna** patterns are painted first on the groom's hands, then on the bride's. Usually, these events take place separately, but sometimes both happen together to save on costs. It is usually a time for the bride to have a party with her sisters and friends.

Nikah or Shaadi

Nikah (nick-ah) or *Shaadi* (shaa-dee) are names given to the actual wedding **ceremony.** First, the legal documents are signed in the presence of a religious official. Then, the religious ceremony takes place. The groom wears a grand turban. The bride wears a brightly colored outfit with a lot of red, and gold jewelry. Once the religious ceremony is over, the man and woman are married.

At this Muslim wedding, the groom wears white, while the bride is wearing lucky red trimmed with gold.

Walimah

Walimah (wal-ee-mah) happens on the third day of the wedding celebrations. It is a great feast given by the groom's family to announce the marriage. Many guests are invited, and the new husband and wife welcome them and visit with them while they are eating.

This Walimah celebration is taking place in Great Britain. The newly married couple talks with guests while they are eating.

Jumilla's story

Jumilla, age seventeen, remembers her sister's *Mehndi* celebrations in Pakistan:

At my sister's wedding, there were lights everywhere, in all the bushes and trees. We set up two tents, one for the men and one for the women. There was singing and dancing. Inside the women's tent we were able to behave in a different way from if it had been in front of everyone.

Imilchil Wedding Festival

Today, in Morocco, about 25,000 people from all over the high Atlas Mountains come to an annual wedding festival in the Imilchil (im-ill-chill) valley. They camp out in the valley for three days. Along with the wedding festival, there is a bazaar where people sell clothes and other goods. On the other side of the camp is a market where donkeys, sheep, and goats are sold.

This girl is one of the Berber people. She is dressed in her finest clothes for the Imilchil festival in Morocco.

The main purpose of the festival is for single people to get married or **engaged.** Few people normally travel from village to village in the mountains, so young men and women do not get much chance to meet. At Imilchil, the women put on their finest clothes and silver jewelry. There is dancing and music, and by the end of the festival many couples are ready to get engaged, even though they may have met only three days before. A **holy** man blesses the couples, and legend says that they will always be happy.

Freedom to choose

An ancient story about a pair of young lovers is told at the Imilchil wedding festival. It tells of two young people who fell in love and wanted to get married. They were from different tribes, though, and their families would not allow it. The young man and woman wept bitterly until their tears made two salty lakes. Their sadness was so great that they drowned themselves in the lakes. After this terrible event, the local people decided that their children were free to marry anyone they wanted.

The groom (dressed in white) meets his bride at the Imilchil festival.

Jewish Weddings

Traditional **Jewish** weddings begin with the bride and groom signing a *ketubah* (kett-oo-bah), or marriage contract. It is usually signed on the day of the wedding. The *ketubah* sets out what the duties and goals of the married couple will be. After it has been signed, the groom lifts his bride's veil, looks at her face, and then lowers her veil.

The wedding ceremony

The wedding **ceremony** begins with a **procession** of all the guests. Once they have reached the place where the wedding will take place, the bride and groom and their parents walk down the **aisle.** The couple is married under a special canopy called a *chuppah* or *huppah*. They make promises to each other and give each other rings, and then **blessings** are read. The bride and groom drink from the same wine glass. The groom then smashes the glass under his foot. This tradition reminds Jews of the destruction of the **Temple** of Jerusalem and how easily human happiness can be destroyed.

This groom at a Jewish wedding is signing the wedding contract, called a ketubah.

Wedding reception

After the ceremony, everyone gathers for eating, drinking, and dancing. This wedding reception is a joyful event. Sometimes the bride and groom are lifted into the air while sitting on chairs. They each hold one end of a handkerchief, and the guests say that they are "king and queen of the night."

This bride and groom at a wedding in Jerusalem have been lifted up in celebration of their marriage.

Rebecca's story

Rebecca Gold, age 16, remembers a family wedding in New York:

At my cousin's wedding they danced a Krenzl because Abigail was the last of three sisters to be married. Her mother sat on a chair in the middle, wearing a crown of flowers. They played a lively song, and all three daughters did a special dance around her.

Buddhism and Shintoism

The **Buddhist** religion is most common in Asia, especially in China and Japan. But, about 300 million Buddhists live throughout the world. Buddhists usually believe getting married has little to do with their religion. There are no special rites that all Buddhists follow when they get married. Instead, they tend to follow the customs of the country in which they live. Once married, Buddhists may visit their local **temple** so that they can be blessed by one of the **monks.**

In Japan, many people still follow the Shinto religion. Shintoism is so old that no one is sure when it began. Its followers believe in *kami* (ka-mee), spirits or gods who live in the Japanese landscape. *Kami* are honored at special shrines, which people often visit during or after important events. One of these important events is a wedding.

This couple in Bangkok makes offerings to Buddhist monks as part of the marriage celebration.

A Shinto wedding is led by a priest called a *kannushi* (kan-oo-shee), who calls to the *kami* to witness the wedding. The couple drinks rice wine called sake (say "saa-kee"), three times to seal the marriage. The bride and groom both wear kimonos (traditional Japanese robes), and the bride wears her hair in a traditional style called *bunkin takashimada* (bunkin tack-ashee-mad-ah).

Traditional costumes are part of this Shinto wedding in Tokyo, Japan. The bride's hair is arranged in a traditional style.

Yukiko's story

Yukiko Shindo describes some Japanese wedding traditions:

In Japan, most people have a party to show their husband or wife to their friends and relatives. Everyone looks forward to seeing the bride's dress. We eat Japanese food that has a special meaning. For example, we eat soba (long noodles), so that the newlyweds will get [along] for a long time.

Native American Weddings

The native people of North America are made up of many different nations. Some have similar languages—the Cree, Chippewa and Montagnais, for example, all speak varieties of the Algonquin (al-gon-kwin) language. Even so, these groups have some customs that are quite different from any others.

Some traditional Native American weddings are small and informal, with little or no **ceremony.** Others have a special ceremony that involves people acting in a certain way. The Hopi Indians, for example, have a set of rules about how a couple becomes married. The marriage must be accepted by both sets of parents. Then, the bride spends three days grinding cornmeal with the groom's mother. (Corn is considered a **holy** food.) His aunts come and "attack" the bride with mud, but the groom's mother defends her. At the end of three days, the couple is bathed. Then, they go to the east to make prayers to the sun. Once these prayers are finished, the couple is married.

Most traditional Native Americans share a belief in some sort of spirit, often called the Great Spirit. The Great Spirit is the source of all life—many people believe that the sun stands for its power. Some Native American weddings, for example those of the Algonquin peoples, ask the Great Spirit to bless the married couple.

Apache wedding prayer

Now you will feel no rain,
For each of you will be shelter to the other.
Now you will feel no cold,
For each of you will be warmth to the other.
Now there is no more loneliness,
For each of you will be companion to the other.
Now you are two bodies,
But there is only one life before you.
Go now to your dwelling place
To enter into the days of your togetherness
And may your days be good and long upon the earth.

This young woman is having a traditional headdress draped over her head. She is taking part in a recreation of a Nisqually Indian wedding.

Mass Weddings

For many people, their wedding is one of the most special days of their life. They are the center of attention, and all of their relatives and friends come to celebrate with them. Other people look at weddings quite differently. They get married in a large group, sometimes with hundreds of other brides and grooms.

One of the most amazing mass weddings ever took place in a **ceremony** held at the Olympic Stadium in Seoul, South Korea, in February 2000. The couples were all members of the Unification Church. The Church is dedicated to building world peace through loving families. Marriage is therefore very important to its members.

The Reverend Sun Myung Moon, leader of the Unification Church, in the middle of a wedding at Madison Square Garden, New York City. Roughly 22,000 couples were married at the ceremony.

Ten thousand North Korean couples were married at the ceremony. Rather than travel to Seoul, people had sent photographs to a center in China. There, they were matched into couples by church officials. The photographs were then sent to Seoul, and a video of the church's leader, the Reverend Sun Myung Moon, was played. In the video, he blessed the couples, and they were then considered married.

Other mass weddings have taken place around the world. In Bahrain in December 2001, 280 couples were married in a ceremony at the Bahrain International Exhibition Center. The weddings were paid for by the emir, the ruler of Bahrain. "This is the last of a group of 1,000 grooms getting married with the emir's help," said his spokesperson. "We aim to help young couples start their life by cutting down on wedding expenses."

Two thousand couples were married at the same time at this mass wedding on New Year's Eve, 1999. The wedding took place in Thailand.

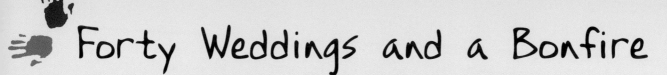

Forty Weddings and a Bonfire

Between the Black Sea and the Caspian Sea in Eastern Europe lies the mountainous country of Armenia. Armenia has close religious links with Russia to the north, and in both countries many people are **Orthodox Christians.**

On February 13, 2002, the tiny village of Karpi, was host to an amazing event. This event was the mass wedding of 40 couples in an Armenian Orthodox **ceremony.** Most came from Karpi itself. So many couples got married that day that the cars that brought them to the church made their own traffic jam.

Brides and grooms parade around the bonfire at Karpi. They waited for the flames to die down before leaping over the embers.

The ceremony for the couples was the traditional Armenian one, and it took place on the 1,700th anniversary of the founding of Christianity in Armenia. The day was also the day of Trndez, a festival in which newly married couples are expected to jump over a fire. A bonfire was built in the churchyard. The brides in their long white dresses waited until it had died down a little before leaping over it. Even so, a few dresses were slightly burned by the fire.

At the end of the day, each couple was given apricot tree seeds to plant. The tree will stand for the start and growth of the couple's family life.

Saint Gregory the Illuminator was responsible for converting King Trdat of Armenia to Christianity in 301 C.E. Armenia became the first country to accept Christianity as its state religion.

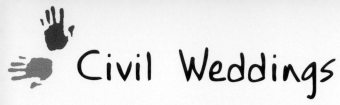

Civil Weddings

In many countries, there are two parts to a wedding. One is the religious part, in which the couple agrees before their god that they will live together and treat each other in a certain way. The second part of the wedding is called a **civil ceremony.** In this, the couple signs legal forms to register with the government that they are married.

In most countries, the civil wedding has nothing to do with religion. If they want to, people can have a civil wedding without any religion being involved. These are usually held in a government office. The man and woman may not have religious beliefs but still want to be married in the eyes of their family, friends, and community. Or, they may want to have children, and they want their children to know that they have promised to stay together. Still other people get married at a civil ceremony because they have been married before. Some religions do not allow people to be married more than once. So if they get **divorced** and then remarry, they cannot have a religious ceremony.

Some people will go a long way to make their wedding a bit different. This couple is getting married underwater, off Key Largo, Florida.

This couple decided to be married on a hillside in the country. Although the bride is in white, it is a civil wedding, not a religious one.

Another reason for getting married at a civil wedding is purely legal. If one of the people in a relationship is from another country, he or she would not normally be allowed to stay in that country permanently. Once they are married, however, a man and woman are usually able to stay together and live in either of their home countries.

Mostly, people get married to show that they want to live together forever. The man or woman they are marrying is very important to them. Winston Churchill, the British prime minister during World War II, showed how important he thought his own marriage was. He said: "My most brilliant achievement was my ability to be able to persuade my wife to marry me."

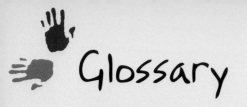

Glossary

aisle walkway or path between two rows of seats

blessing gift or well wishes from God or a holy person

ceremony special ritual and celebration

Christian person who follows the religion of Christianity, which is based on the teachings of Jesus Christ. Christians believe that Jesus was the Son of God.

civil ceremony nonreligious marriage ceremony

divorce legal end of a marriage

engaged term that describes a couple who plan to be married

henna extract of a plant root that is often used to dye skin or hair a reddish-brown color

Hindu person who follows Hinduism. Hindus worship one god (called Brahman) in many forms. Hinduism is the main religion in India.

holy having to do with God or a religious purpose

hymn song in the praise of God

Jew person who follows the religion of Judaism. Jews pray to one god. Their holy book is the Hebrew Bible, sometimes called the Old Testament by Christians.

monk member of a monastery, an all-male religious community. Monks devote their lives to God.

Muslim person who follow the religion of Islam. Muslims pray to one god, whom they call Allah.

Orthodox strict or traditional. Orthodox Christians originally came from eastern and southeastern Europe.

procession people walking together along a route as part of a public or religious festival

Protestant person who believes in a form of Christianity that began in Germany in the 1500s, when Christians first broke away from the Pope's leadership

Roman Catholic Christian who follows the leadership of the Pope in Rome

Sikh person who follows the religion of Sikhism, based on the teachings of the ten Gurus, or teachers

temple building used for worship

vow promise made according to a special set of rules in a ceremony

More Books to Read

Merchant, Karena. *Muslim Festivals.* Chicago: Raintree, 2001.

Miller, Jay. *American Indian Festivals.* Danbury, Conn.: Children's Press, 1996.

Morris, Ann. *Weddings.* New York: HarperCollins Children's Book Group, 1995.

Sonntag, Linda. *Weddings.* Chicago: Raintree, 2001.

Index